NAVREET PABLA

If My Heart Could Talk

POEMS OF
HEALING, HONESTY
AND COMING HOME

Navreet Pabla

If My Heart Could Talk

Poems of Healing, Honesty, and Coming Home

✤ LUCKY BOOK PUBLISHING

Sacred Dedications

To my parents:

Prabhjot Pabla & Mohinder Pabla

Your strength
is a daily reminder
that I, too,
can choose
love
over
hate.

*thank you for doing the best
with what the world gave you.*

To my ancestors:

I carry your love
in every seed I plant,
in every truth I write,
in every life I help.

*we are free now.
and we are endless.*

this book is not a cure.
rather a mirror for your truth,
a map back to your soul,
and a match to light the way.

may it burn away
what no longer belongs to you,
and bless what remains.

Author's Note

To my reader:

If you're here, celebrate yourself.
healing is heavy, but even opening these pages
is proof of your courage.

the words you find here will not always be easy.
some will land like petals.
others may feel like stones.
both will teach you something real and true.

along the way, you may meet pieces of yourself:
the hidden, the forgotten, the ones you've been
waiting for.
let them arrive in their own time.
there is no rush.

you are safe to pause,
to rest,
to laugh in the middle of the ache,
to put these pages down for a day,
a week,
or forever.

this book will wait for you.
and when you return,
it will be right here,
arms open,
ready to walk with you.

My Invitation to You

I'm so glad you're here.

To carry this journey beyond the book,
I created a special bonus chapter called *Dear Body*,
a collection of healing poems to help you rebuild
trust with your body.

This is your invitation to reconnect,
fully and honestly.

Scan the QR code below to receive it for free.

My Dream

I am a poet, yes.
but more than that,
I am a healer,
a guide.
my dream is to see a billion hearts
feel safe enough
to be witnessed,
to be heard,
to come home to themselves.

Somewhere along the way,
I realized these words are not just mine.
they belong to every heart
that has carried the ache of:
a mother wound,
a father wound,
a child left unseen,
an ancestor whispering in the bones,
a heart remembering how to beat unbroken.

My dream is that you remember:
you are not powerless.
you are not alone.

your story is not the end,
it is only the beginning.
and when you finish this book,
you'll rise with courage
to tend the pain that shaped you,
and live guided by your own heart.

My dream begins here:
with you,
with me,
with these words.

Contents

"Every journey home begins with the courage to leave."
– Navreet Pabla

Dear mother

a journey through
grief,
survival,
and trust

I was born from the body
of a woman
who had to carry
too much,
too early.
she never taught me
how to speak,
only how
to stay quiet.
how to bury my anger
until it turned into
blame,
into fire,
aimed
right back at her.

her silence had a history

she left behind
everything she knew,
the language of her land,
the smell of home,
the tender light of youth
to follow a man
she did not choose.

to mother daughters
in a country
that called her voice foreign,
and her strength uneducated.

I didn't know it then,
but my mother had buried
her own mother too early,
lost her girlhood in a breath,
and still chose to mother me
with hands that trembled
from carrying generations.

I didn't understand it then,
I resented the way she worried.
the way she never looked at me
with her full approval.

I mistook her silence
for distance,
her rules
for restriction.

but now I see it:
she gave me the only safety
she knew how to give.

she didn't know
how to nurture.
but she stayed.

that was enough to save me.

my healing truly began
when I chose to see her
not as "mom,"
but as a woman,

a woman with dreams.
a woman who is still
a little girl.

I returned to her,
with eyes wide enough to finally see.

she was never the enemy.
she was the beginning.

now, I carry her
stories as poems.

I write for her,
for every woman
who mothered through mourning,

for the women
who raised daughters
while holding
their own broken hearts
in silence.

this is not just for the mother.
it is for the little girl inside her.
and the little girl inside me.

and for the healing we now
offer each other,
word by word.

dear mama,

your soft skin,
your beautiful gaze,
both carrying the weight
of what was never spoken.

your mother's passing.
your father's silence.
the heaviness your eyes
could never set down.

and still,
you move with a kind of grace
that makes survival
look gentle.

I mistook her silence for strength.
but now I see,
it was endurance.
a choreography of grace
taught by grief
and passed on like a lullaby.

I love you,
for what you carry.
and for all that never broke you.

I wish
I started loving you sooner.

I wish
I noticed all you carried for me.

if I had seen it then,
the way you put me
before yourself,

maybe I would've known sooner:
that my life's greatest
love story
began with you.

~ *you are my first home*

the mother gives
until she is emptied.

she carries and carries,
until the weight settles in her bones,
until exhaustion feels like
her natural state.

she carries stones
that were never meant for her hands
and still her back bends to lift them.

she, too,
is a little girl
learning
to be brave,
to be patient,
to be kind,
to be love.

I see her
not as the mother,
but as a mirror.

and I choose to heal her,
as if healing a wound
in our lineage.

I choose to turn the war we carried
into a peace we can both rest inside.

every act of forgiveness
ripples backward and forward.
through daughters not yet born,
through mothers now gone,
through the silence
our ancestors left behind.

every time
I meet her
with softness
instead of spite,
I am reparenting
us both.

~ *she is me*

mama,

I know you know
everything about me.

yet all I feel is what you
disapprove of.

not once have I heard the words,
I love you.

how could love
live in your mouth
when no one ever
taught it to stay?

still,
I long to hear it,
not for validation,
but because I know
how heavy
it must be
to carry
love.

your hands never spoke,
but they lit the stove,
folded silence
into cloth,
and kept the world from
falling apart.

you gave love
in the language of warmth.
rice waiting patiently,
water rising to a boil,
prayers dissolving
into the steam,
finding their way
into our mouths.

your giving
and your grieving
do not always meet,
but both are holy.

if we've done this before,
I would choose you again,
in every lifetime,
in every silence,
in every form love takes.

the only conversations
I have with my father
are about keeping you safe
because even in silence,
we both know:

you are the piece
holding us together.

your grief wears your skin like silk,
woven from sleepless nights,
unspoken words,
and the weight of what was never said.

and still,
you offer love
like it was never taken from you.
like your light
was always meant to rise.

there are things
we never learned
how to say.

between the lines,
beneath each breath,
I hope you feel it,

we're all just trying
to find our way back
to love.

mama,

with all you've endured,
the way you love me
still feels pure,
still feels true.

you taught me patience
not by saying it,
but by being.

you held the world
when it tried to break you.
with hands that never asked for thanks.

the best gift I can offer
is to see your smile
break through the grief.

and if you can find light
despite it all,
maybe I can too.

you turned me
into the woman.
I am today.

you picked me up
from school each day.
even in college,
you still came,
week after week.

a love so steady,
it taught me patience.

you are braver
than the world ever knew,
than anyone ever gave you credit for.

having learned your pain
I too,
see myself as a reflection of your pain.

I used to carry your pain
like it was a burden.

having touched your wounds,
I finally see,
I am not just your daughter;
I am your mirror.

there were days,
I felt like I was raising you,
and it made me angry.
I didn't want to be your mother
while still needing mine.

I thought you were weak.
but I didn't understand
how strong a woman must be
to keep building walls
with trembling hands,
just to protect the daughter
she could never fully reach.

when did I make you
the villain in my story?

you did nothing
but keep me safe
in the only way you knew how.

it wasn't perfect.
but still,
It was love.

I never realized
your presence
was all I ever needed.

I spent years
naming the cracks,
before I ever thanked
the walls that held me.

and now,
I let the anger melt
into something softer
not because I must forgive,
but because I finally understand
the weight you carried
just to stay.

sometimes love
is not a language
but a presence.
a body showing up
again and again,
even when the words
are missing.

you went from the city
to a village made of dust and duty.

how did you carry humility
into an arranged marriage
into a life you didn't choose,
but chose to honor?

before rest,
the body never forgot
what my mother didn't say.

grief curls beside me now,
not like a wound,
but like someone
who's always lived here.

I did not realize
you were longing for me
every time I would leave.

I tried not to think of you,
it only broke my heart.

now I return
to the emptiness
where my feet once slept,
picking up pieces
of love I didn't know
were always waiting.

it's not your fault.
none of it.

I forgive you,
with the kind of love
that knows
we were both doing our best
with what we were given.

you are my greatest teacher,
my unexpected best friend.

and in another life
if the stars allow,
I hope you are free.
I hope you dance without worry.
I hope you taste joy
without waiting for it to end.

because even in this life,
I would choose you again.
and again.
and again.

I dreamed of you.
happy,
laughing.

and i'm sorry
the world robbed you
of joy.

it took your mother,
then everything else
you called familiar.

you held your grief
so tightly
it became part of your posture.

I wish I had stayed.
close to you.
but I had to leave
to find myself.
to fall apart.
to learn my own name.

I chased men
who could never love me.
ignored your calls,
drowned in parties,
trying not to feel.

I see now:
my resentment
was really longing
in disguise.

I want to know everything about you.
but I don't know where to start.

our conversations feel
so painfully small,
like they're afraid
to open the door
to all the truth
we never got to speak.

but still,
I want to try.

even if all I hear is silence,
I want to listen
until the silence becomes
a song.

thank you
for walking this soul mission
beside me.

if we've done this before,
I hope we do it again.

because even in the silence,
especially in the silence,
I love doing this
with you.

Dear father

A journey through strength, anger, and forgiveness

before he was father,
he was a boy.
before I was woman,
I was his daughter.

his laughter was cut short,
childhood traded
for labor.

he made himself small
to fit into the shape
the world demanded of him.

no one asked what he wanted,
only what he could carry.

his business burned in 1988,
not just trucks,
but the life he was building.

five sisters waited on his back.
a father drowning in drink.
an entire family
balancing on his shoulders.

this loss took everything
from him.
not just the uniforms,
nor just the power,
but the trust,
the sleep,
the skin he lived in.

how does a man return
from a thing
that shakes his world
from the inside out?

dear papa,

sometimes,
I wonder
where you find the strength
to have gone through so much pain,
so much grief,
so much heartache.

your only choice
was to be strong
even when the world
kept burning you down.

you've been to war
with the world
and came back
carrying its bones.

memories of my father & me

as a girl,
I rode his scooter
small hands,
steady heartbeat.

he took me to the farm.
I played in mud,
sand, rocks,
the open dirt,
and felt free.

that was my first love:
not the land,
but the way he held me
without needing to hold me.

I didn't know
his voice
would become the echo
I chased in every man.

I didn't know
I wanted
safety
in the shape
of his sound.

there is no sound
in this world
that holds me
like my father's voice.

I am
my father's first love.

I did not know,
but I know now.

that he too was just a little boy
doing his best
to keep his family safe.

a boy who
learned to protect
before learning
to play.

a boy who
memorized
the sound of duty
before he knew
the sound of laughter.

a boy
who carried everyone
with hands too small
to hold himself.

who became
the roof
before he knew
he was still
the child
under it.

neither of us knew
how to name the distance
we kept
between us.

I always saw it
as a mess of color.
loud,
untamed,
the wild scribble of a
child
hiding her heart
beneath the eyes of a
teacher
who feared beauty
that didn't obey the lines.

~ *my feelings for you*

I've wanted to ask,
are you proud of me?

but that would take effort.
and effort
is something
I've spent years
using
just to stay small.

so instead,
I nod.
I smile.

and I hope you can hear
the thank you
I never learned
to say
out loud.

you never said much,
just set the plate down.
with hands,
too used to giving.

I used to wish for more.
now I wish I'd noticed
how much you gave
without asking
to be seen.

for years,
I painted you
as the bad one,
the shadow in the room,
the presence of punishment.

I needed a villain.
and you were the closest thing I had.

so I called you a monster
and meant it.

how else do you name
the man
whose presence
turned my body to stone.

I've spent years
mistaking your silence for shame,
your anger for punishment,
not knowing it was never about me.

your rage is not yours, is it?

betrayed by your blood,
burned by your own,
taught that love
was something earned
through fear.

you bit down on your rage
until your teeth ached.
until your voice turned to stone.

I will carry your pain
far and wide.
turn it into pure light.

~ *you are so precious to me.*

your anger
is filled
with the deaths you carried,
with grief
you never knew
how to hold.

I remember the day
you learned your father was gone.
his body was oceans away,
and there was no time to grieve.

you went to work instead,
because the bills still waited,
because survival
doesn't pause for sorrow.

I remember the scooter rides,
the wind curling through my hair,
the quiet certainty of your back
steady beneath my hands.

you never told me
how much you worked,
how much you gave up.

but I saw it.
your love was presence,
your love was effort.

you never asked me for anything,
not even when you had nothing.

I thought your silence
meant I was unworthy,
that I was a burden.

but it was never me.
it was the weight you carried,
the losses you endured alone,
the fire within you,
with no place to go.

in the kitchen,
you spoke in spices,
in the sizzle of garlic on oil,
in plates filled before your own.

your glare scared me.
all it ever said was:
don't ask,
don't cry,
don't need.

and yet,
every dish was proof
that love can simmer
even in silence.

sometimes,
I wonder
if the fire in you
was ever meant
to be human.

you've walked through
enough endings
to fill a century,
but still,
you carry the sky
like it belongs to you.

you know how to forgive,
but not how to hold
the betrayal,
the ache of being unseen.

you don't have to carry it alone.
share your pain,
speak it out loud.
only then
will the fire turn
into light.

fire never wonders
if it is too much.
it consumes,
it clears,
it makes way
for beginnings.

~ *your pain, too, is sacred*

your body ached,
your eyes heavy,
but still you rose
each morning
to give the world your hands.

you ate the same food
day after day,
held back from buying
what you longed for,
even gifts from us
felt like a burden.

you carried others first,
and they mistook
your kindness
for weakness.

strength is not hardness.
strength is choosing
to love again,
even when the world
forgot to love you back.

father,
you are worthy
of more than survival.

worthy of love
that does not ask you to shrink,
worthy of money
that does not slip through your hands,
worthy of success
you never have to apologize for.

you do not have to hide.
you do not have to make yourself small.
your worth
was never up for debate.

you are not what you lost.
you are everything
you continue to rise for.

I carry your strength
like stone in my bones,
your resilience
like a drum in my pulse.

for years,
I feared the silence I inherited,
but now I see:
it was a gift.

a father's love

you do not have to become
your father's silence
to honor him.

you are allowed
to speak the words
he could never shape,
to free your throat
from the weight
he kept
beneath the tongue.

your father's shame
is not yours to carry.
lay it down,
like a coat
that never fit your shoulders.

he was a boy
asked to hold too much,
but you,
you are free
to open your hands.

~ *releasing*

my father's hands
are tired, worn,
but still giving,
as if generosity
was the only language
he trusted.

he did not know
how to stop.
and maybe that too
is love.

my father's laughter
was rare,
but when it came,
it sounded like safety
in a bottle,
like for a moment,
the world stopped asking him
to be strong.

may I know rest.
may the tension in me
no longer belong to him.
may the silence
lose its grip.

may I carry forward
only the love,
and leave the weight
where it began.

may I be free.
may that be enough.

I forgive him,
so the chains end here.
his story
does not need to be mine.

I bless his path,
I bless my own.
together,
we walk lighter.

Dear ancestors

A journey through
memory,
devotion,
and return

you are the *breath* of the ancestor
who never stopped believing.

the *dream* that was whispered
long before your name
was ever spoken.

it drifted through generations,
until it found its way home
to you.

it waited

and now,
if you listen between
your heartbeats,
you can feel it rising.

buried deep
in the unseen layers
of your soul,
like a seed tucked
in fertile
earth.

it has waited,
slow as a candle's sigh,
certain as dawn,
for you to remember
it was always here.

the remembering

I have dreamed
with my eyes open,
heart pulled like a tide
toward a voice
I do not remember knowing.

I have woken
with a song inside me
I never learned,
yet it dances on my tongue
like honey from another life.

I didn't grow up
with stories of my
ancestors.

I don't know
their names
or faces.

but I know it's time
and i'm ready
to listen.

what would it mean
for me
to be
the living memory
of someone I've never met?

as the moonlight sings,
the birds begin to dance,
the trees hold smiles,
the flowers laugh.

through you,
I know;
we are the same.
one heart.
holding the ache
of being apart,
and the knowing
we never truly were.

daily, I create
opportunities
to be close to you.

every pattern,
every sign,
every design,
reminds me of you.

every clue was a blessing
dressed as detour,
pulling me closer.

my gratitude
runs deep,
beneath blood,
beneath the bone.

only you
could have given me
the wings
I now use to fly.

the courage
I now use
to thrive.

only you
could have lit this path
long before I knew
to look for it.

and now,
as I walk it,
it speaks
in a language
meant only
for me.

when the silence breaks

no one could've prepared me
for the heartbreaks
woven into my bloodline.

how heartbreak can be braided
into your name.

so much was swallowed.
not even the wind
dared to speak it.

one day,
the silence will break.

and when it does,
I will be there
to listen,
to witness,
to hold
what they couldn't say.

with open arms,
and a gentle embrace,
I will become
the healing
they never had.

I feel the anger
you swallowed whole.
I carry the grief
that pulled you off course.

but I will not heal
by extinguishing the fire.

I will heal
by learning to sit beside it.
by taming the dragon
just enough
to let it guide me.

and with each step,
I return
to the ember
of who I truly am.

the wounds I carry
did not arrive yesterday.

they are the silent truths
left unspoken
by my ancestors.

their unfinished stories
press against my ribs,
waiting to be remembered.

what I once called weight,
I now call wisdom.

how do I explain
this ache to be seen,
wide as the wind,
free as flame,
sharing the messages
you slipped into my soul?

did you always know
you'd be the one
guiding me home?

I travelled to the Ganga river
to throw my grandmother's ashes.
in the water.

weird tradition,
I remember whispering
but even then,
I knew it meant something.

my grandmother
was also a little girl.
I wish I had known her then,
before time stiffened her bones,
before silence took her story.

there's a blur
beyond my grandparents.
shadowed names,
I'd only ever heard once.

sometimes,
I wonder if the answers
were in the river too
carried off
with her ashes.

they say
there was a man
in the mountains
who kept a book
of all my ancestors.
a book of truths,
of bloodlines,
of broken promises
put back together with time.

I believe the book exists.
I believe it carries
the ache I inherited
and the path
I'm learning to walk.

the book has my name, too.

the question is not
whether i'll find the man
in the mountains
but how I'll carry
the book forward myself.

~ sacred waters of the Ganga River

there is anger in my body,
not just mine,
but yours too,
a thousand unshed tears
that called themselves strength.
I speak what you could not,
and heal what you had to hold.

for all of us

I am feeling anger for all of you.
I am feeling grief for all of you.
I get to feel until I free us all.

I get to
feel until I finally break free
from this curse.
I get to heal.
for all of us.

breaking the cycle
is quieter than I thought.

sometimes,
it's just me,
choosing not to yell,
choosing love over pain,
choosing to forgive,
and that's louder
than any scream
I was ever taught.

your voice holds
healing frequencies.
your voice holds
the cries of your ancestors.
your voice carries
your past,
your present,
and all the futures still forming.

every word you speak
vibrates with meaning.
some words
open portals.
some words
rewrite timelines.

your voice is sacred,
so unique
it can only come from you.

it is calling in
people,
experiences,
and moments
that match its tone.

and the power of that tone
is what determines
how the world receives you.

you dreamed
with the dust you were given,
threading starlight
through shadow.

now,
I dream for both of us
on this side of the veil.

I carry the codes
you tucked into silence,
the visions
you buried
in my dreams.

our dreams
are not lost,
they are becoming.

I will walk them
into the light.

to my lineage

I once believed
the path would end
at forgiveness.
but instead,
that is where it began.

I chose the road
few dare to walk.
the quiet way,
the trembling way,
the way back to myself.

and now,
I am awake.

I see it clearly:
the altar
was never outside me.
the crown
was never given.

it grew
from every silence
I dared to break.

I am the prayer
they could not speak
until now.

~ quick awakening

I carry us forward
I take the baton
from your burning palms,
not out of survival,
but destiny.

I stopped waiting
for constellations to align.
I am the light
you whispered into the dark.

my dreams are maps
you buried in my marrow.
finally,
I remember,
what it means
to come home.

speak, child

you come from ancestors
who bent time,
not themselves.
you weren't made to shrink
inside someone else's silence.

they braided
strength into
everything they touched.

you are their unfinished sentence.
your voice is not too loud.
it's the one they've been waiting for.

they swallowed their truth
so you could speak yours whole.
they knelt to survive,
you stand to remember.

you are not the breaking.
you are the bloom
they never got to see.
yet, they know.

they see your beauty
in the way you rise,
in the work you offer,
in every breath
that refuses to dim.

we lit lamps
with cracked hands,
rubbed turmeric
into open wounds,
tied rebellion
into our bangles,
and dreamed you into being
between chants.

now rise,
you are the voice
we buried in silence,
the fire we lit
but never got to see burn.

~ we didn't survive for you
to stay small

lift me with the wings
that carried those before me.
refill this cup
you never let run dry.

may my soul rise
goddess-charged,
ancestor-bound,
forever walking in your light.

with your grace,
I ask.
with your strength,
I move.

today,
as always,
we rise together.

~ ancestral blessing

please share
your sacred grace,
cool the fires
I've yet to face.

surround this home
in quiet flame,
a light that knows
each child by name.

let no ill cross
this threshold line,
your whispered prayers
now woven mine.

bring bounty wide
and joy that stays,
harvested in your ancient ways.

may love
encompass this place
and guide our lineage
gently into rest.

~ *blessings for the home*

thank you
for giving life
to the ones who gave life to me.

they are their own stories,
still unfolding,
and I love them,
just as they are.

~ *my parents*

with you
by my side,
the world
does not seem
so scary.

your patience
teaches me to be kind.
the way you love,
so rare.

how can I ever repay you?

~ thank you for the gift
of a sister

with you
in the room,
I always felt
a little braver.

you didn't say much,
but your presence
spoke safety.

your silence
wasn't distance,
it was grounding.

you taught me
how to stand taller,
not louder.

how do you thank someone
who held you steady
without needing credit?

~ *thank you for the gift*
of a brother

I cannot wait
to become one,
to unite with you.

I know where you are
is filled with love.
but for now,
i'm grateful to be here,
in this wild physical suit.

I can feel the pain.
I can see the contrasts.
this strangeness
this beauty
is so rare.

I love being a magnet
for miracles.
and I know
you're watching me.

how silly it would be
to ignore
the very opportunity
you placed
right in front of me.

Dear inner child

A journey through innocence, forgiveness, and reclamation

dear child,

I know you were afraid.
you cried without sound.
you tried to be small.

but you were never
built to disappear.

the nights were cold.
the hand you needed
never came.

but look,
we made it.

no one carried us.
we walked.

no more shrinking.
no more hush.

we rise,
whole,
brilliant,
louder than shame.

you were never meant
to do this alone.
healing is not a solitary craft.

every piece of you
was shaped
by more than one set of hands:
ancestors humming at your back,
guides steadying the ladder,
me,
here,
listening.

you hand me a sword,
bright as morning.
"cut the ropes," you say,
"the ones that kept us quiet."

you tug my sleeve,
eyes blazing mischief,
and whisper,
"come on,
the world is waiting.
let's go find it barefoot."

suddenly I see it;
healing is not
about mending what broke,
but the rebellion of living
as if we were never ruined.

tea with my inner child

she arrives barefoot,
mud on her ankles,
eyes saddened.

we sip chamomile together.
she tells me
about the nights we cried quietly,
fearing the walls could hear.

I tell her about the mornings now,
how sunlight is the only voice
I answer to.

she laughs,
and the sound
is a door swinging open.

it wasn't always like this.
there were years
when the light passed over me,
when mornings were heavy
with unsung words.

nights sank
into the long shadow of silence.

I learned to hold my breath
like a seed under winter,
waiting
for the season
that would call me home.

there were years
when the light passed over me.
when I felt nothing,
heard nothing,
but the low river of my own thoughts,
carving valleys in the dark.

my story begins
in Abiana Kalan,
Rupnagar,
Punjab.

a small village
held together by the river's thread
and the open hands of the sun.

the first five years
belonged to simplicity:
my mother, my father,
the khet ਖੇਤ where I played,
the schoolhouse,
the home,
the quiet rhythm of days
that felt like forever.

my father worked
from morning to night.

with so little in his pockets,
he still built a world
where my hands never knew
the shape of hunger.

we had little
but enough to share,
enough to laugh
on the good days.

when I was six,
we crossed an ocean
with more hope
than luggage.

canada met us
with cold air and open sky,
a bowl of light
I didn't know
how to hold.

my father
had already been there
six months,
working his hands raw,
saving for a basement
and a small toyota,
both enough
to start a life.

in canada,
the snow came early,
and so did the stares.

I was bullied
for the way my tongue
tripped over the english language,
for the food in my lunchbox,
for not knowing
how to dress myself
in their approval.

I slowly learned
to fold my vowels,
to wear the right shoes,

to tuck away
the girl
who still missed
the grandparents
we left behind.

I didn't know
what it would mean
to leave you behind.

I was six,
too small to imagine
how quiet the house would get
without our laughter
spilling through it.

your world
must have shrunk overnight;
rooms still holding
the shape of our voices,
cups waiting
for hands
that wouldn't return.

I thought I was just moving
across the world.
I didn't know
i was moving away
from yours.

~ grieving the loss of both grandparents,
from overseas

grief did not rush us.
it rooted us,
like the guava tree
in my childhood yard.

in this new world,
your absence tugged
at my sleeve.

like the child in me
still asking,

when do we get to go home?

I left behind
everything i knew.

friends,
teachers,
the house that held
my first everything.

family, too.
whole rooms of love
I would never
sleep inside again.

that's when I learned:
the world doesn't always have words
for the ache we carry.

so it gives us names
that were never ours.

misnamed

they didn't know
what to call it.
the way you glowed,
how your laughter
rose higher than walls
were built to allow.

so they labelled you as:
too much,
too loud,
too proud.

dear inner child,

they called you conceited
when all you were
was sunlight.

I will never bow to that.

your light was never arrogance;
it was truth,
and it scared them.

I choose to honor your path,
not apologize
for the light
that reminds them
of their shadows.

I know
I put you in rooms
where you should have been held.

kept safe.
far from strange hands
and sharp words.

i'm sorry
I wasn't there to protect you.
but I am now.

and all I can say is this:
I love you
with all my heart.
I will never let you go.
I promise.

I am here now,
strong enough
for both of us.

I will not leave you
in the dark again.

together,
we will carve windows
into every wall,
and let the light
find us.

haven

this is the place,
isn't it?

the one we dreamed of
when the dark felt endless.

a window,
a hand,
a light that stays.

wonder,
waiting just for us.

I know
you don't trust this yet.
the quiet,
the open sky.

but stay.

let me show you:
there are mornings
without the weight of running,
nights where the dark
is only
a place to rest.

rest is a key.
and beneath the wreckage,
something long quiet
starts to speak.

you kept me hidden,
but still,
I leaked through.

I craved your attention,
so I curled into your belly,
made a home in your womb.

I miss the days
when I kept you safe.

now, they flinch
when my gold
gleams too close
to their wounds.

~ a love letter from my pain

they call me the activator.
they praised how i turned you
into light.

but they never saw
how long I sat in the dark with you,
learning your language,
learning to survive you.

until you stopped sounding
like danger
and started sounding
like the truth.

~ *to my pain*

dear inner child,

you didn't come here
to carry the weight of the world.
you didn't come here
to fight for space,
to rise like fire.

you came soft.
with a heart open
before your first word.

you came knowing
the language of silence.

and still,
you sang.

~ *I am so proud of you*

some days,
all I know
is how to run
when things get hard.

I hide in notebooks,
scribbling myself
back together.

I hide in glowing screens,
chasing voices
that sound like safety.

I was only a child,
but already,
I was searching
for teachers
who could keep me whole.

I'm sorry
the world made you think
you weren't worthy.

but you are.
you always were.

they couldn't see it,
so you tried to disappear,
tried to earn love
by dimming
your own
light.

worth
was never theirs to give.

it was yours
from the beginning.

still,
I didn't get to be little.
not really.

my body learned to flinch
before it learned to dance.
to freeze
before it could sing.

my childhood was stolen
before I could hold it.

I was seven
when he touched me.
my body froze.
my voice disappeared.
silence
was never consent.

I was touched
and filled with dirt,
with guilt I could not name.

I wanted to run
but where would I go?

my parents worked night shifts,
so my sister and I
were sent to the neighbor's house.

I didn't tell them.
they had enough to carry.
immigrants chasing a dream
that kept slipping away.

the last thing I wanted
was to add my pain
to theirs.

all I wanted
was the power
to say no.

all I wanted
was my voice
to share
the truth.

they say,
"look how strong you've become."

but strength
was never a choice.

don't tell me
I had to go through it
to become who I am.

I was always this
brilliant,
kind,
loud with light.
I didn't need the pain
to prove it.

so yes, i'm angry.
and that anger
is sacred.

it's the child in me
finally saying:
I deserved better.

anger is a holy flame.
if I neglect it,
it burns me raw,
but when I honor it,
it warms my way home.

I learned to
read the room
long before
I ever learned to read.

and now?
I check in with my body
like it's a friend
i'm slowly learning
to trust again.

the body whispers
what memory forgets.

when you silence her crying,
you teach her
her softness is a threat.

you call it strength
when she swallows her needs.
you call it maturity
when she silences her pain.

and one day,
when she apologizes
for asking to be held,
you'll wonder why she keeps falling in love
with people who always leave.

you are not too much.
you were just too bright
for those still learning to see.

all my life,
I was told
I wasn't good enough.

of course I believed them,
I was only a kid.

now their voices haunt me
whenever I step outside
my comfort zone.

but I remind myself:
I can choose
what is true and what is not.
this is *my* story.

I wasn't lazy.
I was a child
tired of carrying storms
too heavy for my hands.

healing is not a race.
it is a garden
that blooms
when it's ready.

they taught you
to rush.
to build walls.
to fold your magic
so no one would flinch.

but still,
you kept blooming
in the cracks.

before you armor up,
remember,
you were made for warmth,
not war.

when I look at you,
I see the world.
its wonder,
its wild,
its sky-colored light.

blue and yellow fill the room
like laughter without reason.

the way you love should be a crime.
so reckless,
so holy.

your heart is so pure,
I thank the stars it's ours.

inner child,

you're amazing.
yes, you.
I love your two braids,
the way you dress for school
like it's a celebration.

your joy is radiant,
your creativity unstoppable.
you make beauty
out of anything.

resourceful,
resilient,
incredible.

and then together

we return to the earth.
pressing our palms into the soil
to feel her heartbeat
beneath our own.

we offer her the weight
we no longer wish to carry,
and in return
she gives us roots.
steady, unshakable,
strong enough
to grow again.

from here,
I give myself better.

I hold my own hand,
speak my own name
like a blessing.

I make sure the child in me
never wonders again.
she is,
and will always be,
loved.

Dear heart

A journey through belonging, heartbreak, and homecoming

I walk in,
you're already waiting.
legs crossed,
high heels slicing the air.

you smell like flowers,
look like trouble,
and throb like the promise
of something delicious.

you ache to be seen.
childlike,
beneath a queen.

I laugh,
because even here,
I can feel you tugging me
toward the next wild thing.

you've been
shameless and sacred,
both at once.

you've made me
fall in love
with strangers and cities,
with moments that led me
nowhere.

you've broken me open
for moments
that dissolved like smoke.
and still,
I would follow you.

again,
and again.

I cannot believe
how strong you are.

you outlived the fifteen-year-old
who stared at her phone
all day, all night,
waiting for a text from friends
who were laughing
without her.

you buried the girl
who learned at seventeen
that love can lie straight to your face.

and still,
you beat
like you've never been split open.

how dare the heart
love like that.
how beautiful
that it does.

you've carried me
farther
than I dreamed.
even across the world,
to a place called Indonesia.

just to see
if the horizon
would taste different
when I chased it alone.

you were right.

the air was heavy
with possibility.
and my laugh,
for the first time in years,
sounded like it finally
belonged to me.

even when
I wanted
to stay broken,
you leaned close,
whispered
the bigger picture
into my ear.

you reminded me:
the world keeps turning,
and so must I.

you held me in both hands
and said:

even this
is part of the story
we are here to tell.

you've been reckless with love,
and still,
you've been right.

you've handed yourself
to people
who didn't know
how to hold a thing
that beats this loud.

to people with hands
that didn't know
how to hold a
thing so precious.

you've traded hours,
sleep,
and dreams meant for me
just to keep their eyes on you.

yet you stayed loyal
for something bigger
than anyone could ever give.

one day, I'll tell the world
about the things
you and I
create,
when no one's looking.

how you bloom for me
when no one's watching.

dear heart,

I just want to stay close,
feel your pulse against mine.
you don't abandon.
you don't betray.
you turn even the simplest
moments
into true divinity.

but dear heart,
you've always
chased the spark,
even when it flared and vanished,
even when it gave you
nothing but smoke
in return.

you mistook the warm glance
for a promise,
the steady hand
for a home.

you poured yourself
like wine into an unsteady glass,
hoping the moment
would be strong enough to hold you.

you lingered at doorways
built for wanderers,
forgetting that some footsteps
are never meant
to circle back home.

it was the first fall,
and loving him felt so right.
we were two kids
falling in love
without a care in the world.

but you,
you've always leapt
before I could tell you
to slow down.

he changed my life,
and I thought
I could change his.

some things
are not meant
to be changed,

only admired
for the way they were
before you ever arrived.

ex-lovers

my heart picked you
before I knew
what picking meant

before my body ached,
before I
could spell regret.

then came the mind,
with her careful questions
and quiet what ifs.

if she had spoken first,
I would've walked.

but my heart is foolish.
she dances barefoot
on broken clocks.
and she said yes
before the rest of me
could say anything else.

if my heart could talk,
I know it would say:
"I wish you stayed."

I should've known
the first time
he slammed the door
hard enough
to make the picture frames
shake.

I should've known
when my words
became a little too quiet,
just to keep the peace.

but you, heart,
you stayed.
you believed him
when he said
he didn't mean it.

you searched his anger
for the boy
who once dreamed
of being gentle.

if you had let me,
I would have walked away.
not empty,
not bitter,
but with both hands
full of the love
you never learned to hold.

I would have chosen myself
before you ever mistook
my presence
for a promise
you never meant to keep.

I never needed you to change.
because I,
I was already becoming
the woman I was meant to be.

I never needed you to love me.
because I had to learn
the fiercest love of all
was already waiting
inside of me.

dear heart,

you've always been loyal
to the wrong kind of hunger.

a flicker of hope
still pulls me forward.

the world
lures you into places
you never imagined,
sets before you landscapes
and bright ideas
you can't resist.
then it takes them back,
leaving only the hollow
that turns into the lesson.

~ *starting over*

look at you now,
standing at the doorway
of your own life,
palms open,
ready to feed yourself
before you starve
on someone else's love.

now the air is lighter,
and what belongs to you
will find its way in.

I am both the wound
and the woman
who grew around it.

I'm in no rush.
I'm safe being right here,
resting in the quiet,
letting peace hold me
before chaos comes
knocking again.

until then,
I'll sit,
and I'll watch the horizon,
thinking of what it could have been
if we had given ourselves a chance.

and when grief finally comes,
I set a cup before it,
letting the steam rise
between my trembling hands.

in the quiet,
it tells me its name is teacher,
and I let the truth of it
seep all the way in.

the return

give them space.
they'll figure it out.
they're also doing this
for the first time.

we're all here to learn,
sharing one heart.

who's to say who's better?
we're all one.

and still
I keep learning
that the one heart
I'm most responsible for
is my own.

dear heart,

I am not behind.
I am right on time.

my devotion is enough.
my creations unfold
in divine rhythm.

when I move with clarity,
the path clears before me.
I trust
that what is mine
will never miss me.

I've learned,
there is nothing to chase,
only what I choose
to meet halfway.

I am tired of running.
I want to rest,
to feel at peace
here,
in your arms.

your presence
does not push me away.
It presses against me
to show me
all I have refused to see.

I am ready now,
ready to hold you close
and speak the secrets
I once swore
I'd carry to the grave.

~ I surrender
to my truth

dear heart,

I wish you kept me safe
from broken men.

but maybe you were busy
trying to keep yourself alive.

for years
I thought healing meant
changing you.

but it was never you
that needed fixing.
it was the way
I refused to look.

one day,
I picked up a mirror,
met a face
I'd never fully seen.

bare, but burdened.

loved by family,
and most cruelly;
judged by me.

I didn't realize
how heavy the mirror was
until I set it down.

I'm beyond grateful
that you chose me
to be in this human body,
to pump strong
even after all the abuse.

you've gone through so much
and I love you for that.

it's okay to rest now.
it's okay to hand me the wheel
and let yourself be held.

you're only temporary, too,
and I want every beat you give me
to feel free.

~ *gratitude in the body*

the way you love
is like nothing I've ever known.

the way you nudge me
to smile at a stranger
in the grocery store.

why would I do that?
because I want to be kind,
says you.

and as much as I hate it,
I smile,
and I say hello too.

you're always searching
for the smallest cracks
to plant grace,
always finding ways
to leave the world softer
than you found it.

of course life loves me.
look at what it does for me.
look at what it gives me.

it gives me opportunities to grow.
it gives me pain,
so I will know
the shape of love.

it gives me freedom,
so I can see
I was always safe in confinement,
that even the cage
was a kind of shelter.

I heal my heart
by sending it prayers.
it grows bigger
and bigger,
until it overflows
into every corner
of my life.

what was once a wound
is now a well,
and I drink from it daily.

dear heart,

I am here now.
no longer chasing
what cannot hold me,
no longer starving
in rooms where I bring the feast.

you are my first shelter,
my truest country,
the place I return to
even when I have wandered
too far to see the map.

~ *coming home*

we walk together now,
you and I,
without the constant tug-of-war.

you point,
and I listen.
I slow,
and you trust me.

this is how we were always
meant to move.
not as strangers
sharing a body,
but as companions
carving the same road.

everything was for this

every wrong turn,
every goodbye,
every sharp edge
I pressed my hand against
just to feel something,

it was all pointing me here.
to the quiet joy
of knowing I am whole,
to the holy peace
of not needing to be found.

I promise you,
dear heart,
we will not forget this.

we will not forget
how we made a home
from the rubble,
how we lit our own path
when the sun refused to rise.

we will not forget
that our love for each other
is the first and last truth
we ever needed.

healing is not a finish line.
it's a table you set
for yourself every morning,
whether or not you feel hungry.

some days
you will sit in silence.
some days
you will feast.

either way,
you are fed.

your heart will begin to speak
in languages you thought were lost.
joy without condition,
love without measure.

the air itself will lighten.
your body will remember
what it means to be home.
even your shadows
will stay,
because here,
they are safe too.

this is the vow:
to never leave yourself again.
and that is how
you come home.

one day,
you will wake up
and realize
there is no "back" to go to,
only forward,
only here.

your story
will not be a map of what you endured,
but a record of what you chose,
again and again,
to become.

and the sky,
as if in agreement,
will open.

if you are reading this,
know that your heart
has been waiting for you
since the first breath.

and when you finally arrive,
it will not ask
why it took you so long.

it will not tally
the years you were gone
or the places you wandered
looking for a home
that was never anywhere else.

it will only open the door
and say,
"you're here.
come in.
I've been saving your seat."

"Starchild,
you were the key all along."
- Navreet Pabla

Acknowledgements

This book is dedicated to my parents,
who to this day continue to support me and
my dreams.
For years, I judged, resisted, and even feared the
love they offered.
It took heartbreak after heartbreak
to finally see them clearly
and to become whole.

To everyone who held me through the storms and
the silences, thank you.
To my family and friends, who gave me more
patience than I gave myself, thank you.
To my teachers and guides, seen and unseen, who
placed words in my hands when I thought
I had none left, thank you.
And to you, the reader,
thank you for sitting with these pages,
and for letting my heart meet yours.

About the Author

Navreet Pabla is a poet and storyteller.

Today, she shares her insights not only through poetry, but also as a speaker and workshop leader, guiding conversations on ancestral healing, community building, inner child work, creativity, and spiritual growth.

This is her *first* book, but not her last.

Navreet Pabla writes from the intersection of heartbreak and healing. Her words are rooted in honesty, vulnerability, and the long journey of learning to come home to herself. When she isn't writing, she is listening; to her body, to the earth, and to the stories that shape us.

Her writing has grown from years of personal reflection and transformation, and now serves as a companion for others on their own path toward homecoming.

she continues to write, create, and share from a place of truth and compassion.

Connect with Navreet:
Instagram: @navreet.pabla
Website: www.navreetpabla.com
Email: hello@navreetpabla.com

My Invitation to You

I'm so glad you're here.

To carry this journey beyond the book,
I created a special bonus chapter called *Dear Body*,
a collection of healing poems to help you rebuild
trust with your body.

This is your invitation to reconnect,
fully and honestly.

Scan the QR code below to receive it for free.